BTS
DYNAMITE
THE STORY OF THE SUPERSTARS OF K-POP

Written by Carolyn McHugh

sona
BOOKS

© Danann Media Publishing Limited 2021

First published in the UK 2021 by Sona Books an imprint of Danann Media Publishing Ltd.

WARNING: For private domestic use only, any unauthorised Copying, hiring,
lending or public performance of this book is illegal.

CAT NO: SON0502

Photography courtesy of

Getty images:

- Jeff Kravitz/FilmMagic
- Chris Polk
- The Chosunilbo JNS/Imazins
- THE FACT/Imazins
- JTBC PLUS/Imazins
- Han Myung-Gu/WireImage
- ilgan Sports/Multi-Bits
- Kevin Winter
- Big Hit Entertainment/AMA2020
- YOAN VALAT/AFP

- Rich Fury
- Kevin Winter/AMA2017
- Kevin Mazur/WireImage
- Chelsea Guglielmino
- Chris Polk/AMA2017
- C Flanigan
- ROBYN BECK/AFP
- The Chosunilbo JNS/Imazins
- THE FACT/Imazins
- YOAN VALAT/AFP

Other images Wiki Commons

Book layout & design Darren Grice at Ctrl-d
Editor Tom O'Neill

All rights reserved. No Part of this title may be reproduced or transmitted in any material form
(including photocopying or storing it in any medium by electronic means and whether or not
transiently or incidentally to some other use of this publication) without the written permission
of the copyright owner, except in accordance with the provisions of the Copyright, Designs
and Patents Act 1988.Applications for the copyright owner's written permission should be
addressed to the publisher.

This is an independent publication and it is unofficial and unauthorised and as such has no
connection with the artist or artists featured, their management or any other organisation
connected in any way whatsoever with the artist or artists featured in the book.

Made in EU.
ISBN: 978-1-912918-67-6

CONTENTS

MEET BTS 8

INTRODUCING THE BOYS 18

K-POP AND ITS IDOLS 34

TEAMWORK MAKES THE DREAM WORK 38

MAKING MUSIC 48

LIVE SHOWS AND APPEARANCES 60

BTS ARMY MARCHES ON 78

FASHION FORWARD 84

DOING GOOD AND GIVING BACK 96

WINNERS 104

For the first time since the birth of rock and roll in the USA more than 60 years ago, Western pop music's world domination is being challenged. Leading the charge are the seven shining South Korean stars who form the K-Pop phenomenon BTS – the highest grossing boy band in the world.

In just a few years the BTS boys - RM, Suga, J-Hope, Jin, Jimin, V and Jungkook - have built on their success in their South Korean homeland to storm the charts around the world. They have chalked up sales of more than 10 million albums, made number one on iTunes charts in more than 65 countries, topped the US Billboard Social 50s chart for 114 weeks and completed a US stadium tour and a sell-out world tour. They are the first South Korean group to have performed at, and been nominated for, a US Grammy award. In 2019 BTS made Time magazine's list of Most Influential People.

Comparisons with The Beatles abound – they are the first group since those '60s icons to have achieved three number one albums in less than a year. Similarly they have an incredible and devoted fan base. Beatlemania actually has nothing on the fandom that is the BTS Army.

MEET

BTS perform onstage during the 2018 Billboard Music Awards at MGM Grand Garden Arena on May 20, 2018 in Las Vegas, Nevada

8

The name BTS comes from the Korean word Bangtan Sonyeondan, which translates as 'Bulletproof Boy Scouts'. The BTS boys chose this to exemplify their aim of 'blocking out stereotypes, criticisms and expectations' which can reign down on teenagers and young adults 'like bullets'.

Many of their self-penned songs follow this theme – helping young people to withstand the pressures and problems of modern society which can impact on their mental health.

Since July 2017, BTS has said that their name now also stands for 'Beyond The Scene' to reflect the fact that their fans are moving forward by overcoming the realities they face.

But don't be fooled into thinking that their music is therefore mournful and introspective. Quite the reverse. The boys want their sound to lift people up and give them energy and self-confidence – think rap, hip hop, pop and EDM (electric dance music). Now add some of the slickest, tightest, most elaborate choreography around. One look at a BTS video will show you why they have become a global force to be reckoned with.

BTS BIRTHDAYS AND STAR SIGNS

RM 12 September 1994 – Virgo
making him clever, fastidious and modest

Suga 9 March 1993 – Pisces
making him imaginative, compassionate and loving

J-Hope 18 February 1994 – Pisces
making him imaginative, compassionate and loving

Jin 4 December 1992 – Sagittarius
making him optimistic, generous and playful

Jimin 13 October 1995 – Libra
making him artistic, fair and sociable

V 30 December 1995 – Capricorn
making him committed, responsible and serious

Jungkook 1 September 1997 – Virgo
making him clever, fastidious and modest

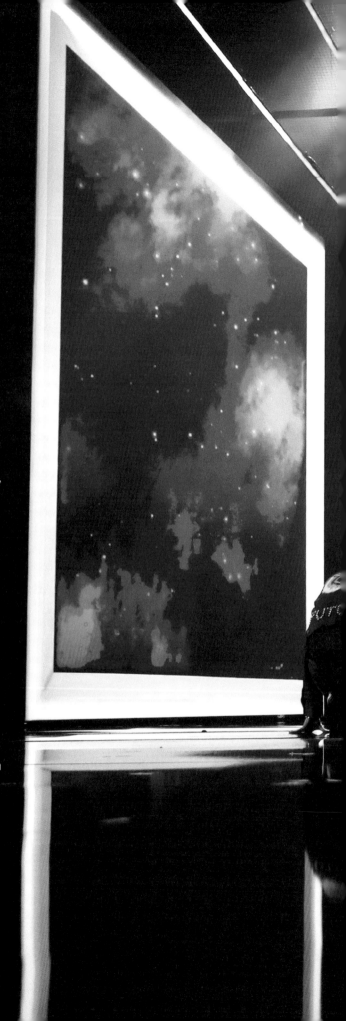

Friend of the band, Grammy-nominated singer/song writer Halsey, describes them as 'outwardly polished and professional, but hours of laughter, secret handshakes and gifts exchanged show those around them that underneath this show-stopping, neatly-groomed movement are just some guys who love music, one another and their fans'.

The boys are also heavily involved with charities and have become worthy role models for their legions of fans.

'We came together with a common dream to write, dance and produce music that reflects our musical backgrounds, as well as our life values of acceptance, vulnerability and being successful,' group leader RM said in a 2017 interview with Time magazine.

BTS stand out from the K-Pop crowd by writing their own material which has socially - conscious lyrics, creating and managing most of their own social media, focussing on albums rather than singles, and talking openly to fans about their own personal struggles in life.

This all combines to give them an incredible allure which has accelerated their ascendency into Western mainstream music .

BTS perform 'DNA' onstage during the 2017 American Music Awards at Microsoft Theater on November 19, 2017 in Los Angeles

BTS perform onstage during their 1st album "Dark&Wild" showcase at Blue Square on August 19, 2014 in Seoul, South Korea

BTS

BTS
TIMELINE

2012

2013

2014

2015

2016

Opened a Twitter account to kick off communication with their fans

First hit single 'No More Dream'

Skool Luv Affair album makes No 3 on US Billboard chart

I Need U gives BTS its first music show win – SBS MTV's 'The Show' – since their debut performance

Achieve first Album of the Year at Melon Music Awards with Young Forever

2018

2019

2017

2020

BTS become first South Korean band to win a Billboard music award, beating acts such as Justin Bieber and Selena Gomez to become 'Top Social Artist'

BTS enjoy their first No 1 on the US Billboard 200 chart with Love Yourself – the first ever K-pop album to top the American chart Launch 'Love Myself' campaign with UNICEF to end violence against children

Make first appearance at the US Grammy Awards show when they present artist H.E.R with the prize for Best R&B album

smash hit Dynamite – the band's first single sung in the English language – shoots to No 1 on the US Billboard Hot 100 chart and reaches Number 1 in the UK

BTS is nominated for its first Grammy Award for 'Pop Duo/Group performance'

17

INTROD

THE BOYS

JIN vocalist and visual

V lead dancer, vocalist

J-HOPE main dancer, rapper, sub-vocalist

Meet the seven superstars of BTS. The talented septet who live and work together, co-writing and producing much of their music. They describe themselves as 'friends, business partners and roommates'.

RM leader, rapper

SUGA lead rapper

JIMIN main dancer, lead vocalist

JUNGKOOK main vocalist, lead dancer, sub-rapper

19

BTS LEADER AND RAPPER

RM is the leader of the boys – the whole band was essentially built around him – and, because he has the most fluent English, he's the one who usually acts as the main spokesman in interviews and personal appearances.

Born **Kim Nam-jun** in South Korea on 12 September 1994, RM grew up with his younger sister in the Ilsan-gu area which is less than 20 miles from the capital Seoul.

Top US sitcom Friends is responsible for RM's great English language skills. His mother bought him the complete box set and he watched all 10 series, first with South Korean subtitles, then with English subtitles and then with no subtitles at all.

RM's interest in hip hop and rap began when he was aged 11 – particular influences were Epik High and Eminem. As a teenager, he began rapping in local amateur hip hop circles and went on to record one of his own compositions. Using the name Runch Randa, RM became increasingly active in the underground Korean hip hop scene and began to get noticed, eventually coming to the attention of Big Hit CEO Bang Si-hyuk who invited him to join his Big Hit Entertainment studio as an idol trainee in 2010 when RM was 16.   Working with his producer Pdogg, Bang had the idea of building a hip hop group around RM and this eventually became idol group BTS.

During his time at the studio RM used the stage name Rap Monster which had been coined by fans. But he now prefers the abbreviation 'RM' as he believes 'Rap Monster' is no longer representative of who he was or the music that he creates. As he has said in interviews, 'RM could symbolize many things. It could have more spectrums to it', including "Real Me".

RM trained for three years with fellow BTS members Suga and dancer J-Hope. He arrived with no dance experience and worked hard to improve his moves. His singing voice is described as baritone, meaning it has weight and power and a very masculine sound. His leadership is particularly apparent when the band are in the studio as he writes and produces much of their music.

While he was training at Big Hit, RM wrote the explicitly pro-LGBTQ song Party XXO which was the debut single for girl group Glam. The track was praised by Billboard as "one of the most forward-thinking songs out of a K-pop girl group in the past decade."

Now RM produces and writes lyrics for many tracks on all BTS albums. He performed the introductory track to the BTS EP O!RUL8,2?.

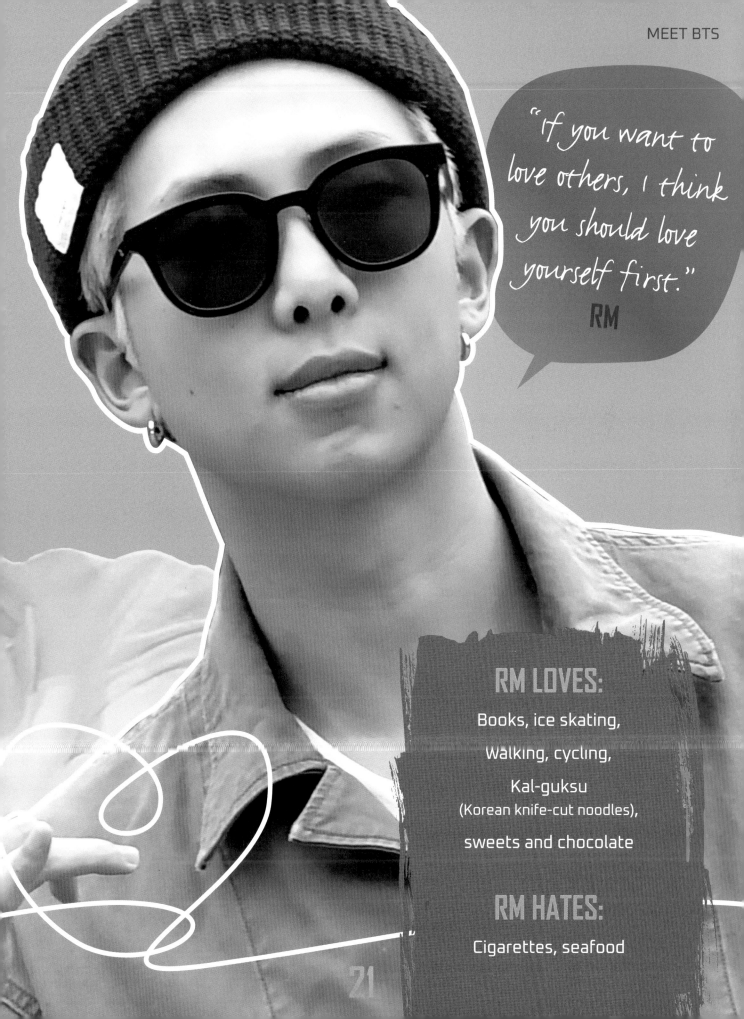

"If you want to love others, I think you should love yourself first."
RM

RM LOVES:

Books, ice skating,

Walking, cycling,

Kal-guksu
(Korean knife-cut noodles),

sweets and chocolate

RM HATES:

Cigarettes, seafood

LEAD RAPPER

Suga is the stage name of **Min Yun-ki**, one of the band's lead rappers. The name Suga is said to come from the first syllables of the words 'shooting guard' which was the position he played in basketball as a student. However, many fans say it is because he is sweet as sugar.

He was born on 9 March 1993 in Daegu, South Korea, the younger of two sons. Inspired by rappers such as Stony Skunk and Epik High, he developed his interest in hip hop and rap and began to write his own material when he was around 13 years old.

By the time he was 17 he had got a part-time job at a record studio and things went well from there as he started doing more composing and arranging music. He also took the chance to develop his talents for rapping, performing, producing, mixing and mastering his material.

Much like RM, Suga was already a popular underground rapper when he first signed with Big Hit as a music producer. As well as making a name for himself as an underground rapper known as 'Gloss', he was part of the hip hop crew D-Town.

He trained under Big Hit Entertainment alongside RM and J-Hope for three years before making his debut.

He has produced and written lyrics for a variety of tracks on all of BTS' albums. The Korea Music Copyright Association credits him with more than 70 registered songs.

As well as his stage name of Suga, he also uses the alias Agust D, which is derived from the initials DT, short for his home Daegu Town, mixed with the word 'Suga' spelled backwards. For example when he released his self-titled mixtape in 2016 it was credited to Agust D.

As one of the oldest members of BTS, he is something of a father-figure to the younger members of the band.

22

SUGA LOVES:

Playing the piano
basketball, meat,
fancy headphones

SUGA HATES:

Noisy, busy places
full of people

23

MAIN DANCER, RAPPER, SUB-VOCALIST

J-Hope is the stage name chosen by **Jung Hoseok**, the group's main dancer/choreographer and an accomplished rapper.

He chose to incorporate 'hope' into his name because he wants to be a source of hope to his bandmates and their fans.

J-Hope was born in Gwangju, south-west South Korea, where he lived with his parents and elder sister. Before signing with Big Hit Entertainment as a trainee idol when he was 15, he had taken dance classes for six years, winning various local and national prizes and becoming part of the underground dance team Neuron. J-Hope's dance style is influenced by street and freestyle hip hop dance — he's upbeat and energetic, with precise poppin' and lockin' moves. BTS are acknowledged as having some of the most complicated choreography in K-pop.

J-HOPE LOVES:

Making a noise,
shopping in NY's Soho district,
puppies, Sprite,
kimchi, lollipops

J-HOPE HATES:

Working out, snakes,
roller-coasters
and feeling scared

25

VOCALIST AND VISUAL

Nicknamed **'Worldwide Handsome', (WWH for short), Jin** is the eldest boy in the group and the official 'visual' member.

Born on 4 December 1992 in Anyang, Gyeonggi-do, as **Kim Seok Jin**, he moved to Gwacheon, near the capital city of Seoul, when he was just a year old. He has one brother, two years his senior, called Kim Seok Joong.

He was well travelled even before hitting the road as a pop star because his father was a company CEO who took Jin with him on business trips. Jin also spent a year in Australia as an exchange student during his middle school years.

In summer 2011, just three months after joining Konkuk University to study acting, Jin was spotted by a scout from Big Hit and offered a number of opportunities. But he eventually chose to join BTS, alongside RM, Suga and J-Hope who were already in place.

In his spare time, Jin enjoys cooking. In April 2018, he worked with his brother to open a restaurant in Seoul, near Lake Seokchon, called 'Ossu Seiromushi'. It specialises in steamed Japanese dishes.

As the eldest member of BTS Jin is happy to act as a mentor to the other members, who tease him by refusing to laugh at his 'dad jokes' and calling him 'omma', which means 'mum' in South Korean.

26

> "Those who want to look more youthful should live life with a young heart."
> JIN

JIN LOVES:

Tennis, swimming, golf & snowboarding, strawberries,

sugar gliders
(nocturnal gliding possums),

lobster & Korean cold noodles
known as Naengmyun.

JIN HATES:

Horror movies,

bugs landing on his body.

BTS

JIMIN

LEAD DANCER & VOCALIST

Dance king **Jimin** is known for his work ethic and competitive side and describes himself as a perfectionist.

He was born **Park Ji-Min**, in Geumjeong, Busan, on the south-east coast of South Korea where he lived with his parents and younger brother.

Before joining Big Hit he had studied contemporary and modern dance and did so well that teachers suggested he audition for an idol studio, which he did successfully with Big Hit in 2012.

His singing voice adds a high range to the group's sound.

EARLY LIFE

JIMIN LOVES:

Mochi, relaxing, meat,
fruit (except mangoes) and
kimchi jjigae, his six pack,
caps and bandanas,
comic books, eyeliner, jewellery.

JIMIN HATES:

Mangoes, spinach.

29

VOCALIST, VISUAL.

V was born **Kim Tae-hyung**, in Daegu, South Korea and grew up, with his younger brother and sister, in Geochang County. He says that his stage name V stands for the word 'victory'.

He took singing and saxophone lessons as a child and became a trainee idol with Big Hit Entertainment in 2011 aged 17. He is highly praised for his 'deep and husky' singing voice, but has also worked hard enough to make the dance line within the band.

In 2016, V made his acting debut with a supporting role in the South Korean television historical drama 'Hwarang: The Poet Warrier Youth'.

A songwriter and producer as well, he also has an interest in photography, he told TIME magazine.

EARLY LIFE

V LOVES:

Popcorn, New York, photography, fashion - especially Gucci, classic & jazz music, potato pancakes & amusement parks

V HATES:

Cooking, coffee, alcohol.

VOCALIST, DANCER & SUB-RAPPER

Jungkook is the youngest member of the group, having been born **Jean Jeong-guk** in 1997. Like Jimin, he's from the southern port city of Busan on South Korea's south east coast, where he lived with his parents and elder brother.

He was a strong badminton player but decided he wanted to be a singer when he was 14 and auditioned for the South Korean talent show Superstar K in 2011. Although he didn't win the contest, the exposure got him noticed and he went on to receive offers from seven big K-Pop studios. But he turned them all down in favour of joining the idol training programme at Big Hit Entertainment, and BTS, reportedly because he was a such a big fan of RM.

EARLY LIFE

JUNGKOOK LOVES:

Banana milk, gaming, popcorn, drawing, soccer, shoes, makeup

JUNGKOOK HATES:

Tasteless things, bugs, getting hurt, studying.

K-Pop – short for Korean Pop – is essentially South Korea's take on Western pop; a mash up of different styles including electronic, hip hop, pop, rock, R&B and rap – all brightly lit and with the dial turned up. It's an ever-changing genre which tends to be more experimental than western music – songs can surprise listeners by taking off in unexpected directions.

It's super-catchy, high-energy, creative and dynamic.

P

The phenomenon dates back to 11 April 1992, when a hip hop trio called Seo Taiji and Boys appeared on a South Korean talent show. The group was a 'New Kids on the Block-style' boy band – very different to the acts which had gone before it, challenging norms of the time with their choices of song topics and style.

They struck a chord with viewers and became a huge hit, going on to become the most successful band in South Korean music history of that time. Their first song spent 17 weeks at No 1 and kickstarted the phenomenon that is K-Pop.

Seo Taiji's rise to prominence came at a good time – they were fortunate that their success coincided with the South Korean government becoming more democratic and relaxing its previously tight control of music production. Now, instead of condemning music, the government felt inclined to support it, seeing it as a marketable export.

Quick to seize on the potential of this new music, several South Korean studios began to develop what were called 'idol' groups during the 1990s. Essentially each studio created its own stars, using a system of auditions and then putting the chosen few through an intensive course of rigorous training.

Children audition from any age after 11 upwards and, if chosen, become trainee 'idols' – perfectly polished pop stars. The trainees live and learn together in a boarding

IDOLS

BTS 2013, Hallyu Dream Concert, October 5, 2013, Gyeongju, South Korea

school-type set up called an academy, perfecting every note sung and move made. Apart from natural talent, the trainees need to have grit and a good work ethic. It's hard work, days are long, sometimes up to 14 hours, with just one day off a fortnight.

The emphasis is on vocal and dance training, with endless repetition ensuring that the trainees' muscle memory becomes automatic. By the end of their time at the studio school, the trainees are equipped with all the tools and techniques to become a successful idol – although not all will make the grade.

Most have moved away from their families and homes in order to take up the idol training opportunity and so loneliness can be the first hurdle to overcome.

Sometimes they will study at idol school for years, while others who join later might only be there a few months before making their 'debut'. Some never debut at all, having been eliminated if they receive a low grade at the regular monthly performances. At these vital shows, each trainee will be graded on their performance as a soloist and within a group – the groups are regularly recast as the studios try out different line-ups and formats.

Once passed as an 'idol', the studio will try each boy or girl out in different groups to see which work best. When everyone has their right place and role, big things can happen – think stage school meets X Factor and American Idol and add Olympic standards competition for good measure.

K-Pop has become huge through this system, gaining popularity in other Asian markets, particularly Japan. But one market was seemingly impossible to crack – the behemoth that is the Western pop world of the UK and America. At the time BTS was formed, not one South Korean artist had managed to gain any traction at all in the west. Fame in America seemed a distant dream. But all that was about to change ......

While the BTS boys were still at school and could only dream of making it in the music business, the man who was to become their mentor was already making a name for himself in the South Korean music industry.

Bang Si-hyuk was a top music arranger and producer working for one of South Korea's leading music companies when he decided to set up his own studio in 2005. He called his new venture Big Hit Entertainment and set himself the mission of doing things differently, to help his trainees succeed without excessive pressure. He already had the nickname 'Hitman' because of his track record, but even he could scarcely have believed how his new company would thrive.

He was looking for young talents with an edge – and one of his first signings was RM who had already gained a name as part of South Korea's underground rap scene, rather than coming up through the established idol system. Bang first thought to promote RM alone, with a supporting crew around him, but eventually decided to use him as part of a more traditional 'idol' boy band. Bang is quoted as saying that he had decided that the contemporary youth needed instead 'a hero who can lend them a shoulder to lean on, even without speaking a single word'. That's how BTS was born.

The rest of the band was put together by the Big Hit Entertainment audition process. While still focussing on rappers, Suga and J-Hope were the first additional signings, then over the next few years different styles and combinations were tried

 Rap Monster at a fanmeet in Cheongnyangni on July 6, 2013

before the BTS line-up was reorganised and expanded to include four new talents; Jin, V, Jimin and Jungkook.

Evidently every one of the boys is a talented singer, dancer, songwriter and performer. However, in common with many South Korean acts, generally the performers will have a speciality and work in subgroups, or 'lines' for the most challenging vocals and dances. With BTS being less staged than other groups, its roles are more blurred, but the usual 'rap line' is RM, Suga and J-Hope, the 'vocal line' is Jungkook, V, Jimin and Jin and the 'dance line' is J-Hope, Jimin and Jungkook. There is also a role called 'visual' relating to good looks, charm and appeal. Again while this applies to all the BTS band, their official 'visual' is Jin, with V and Jungkook now also getting a lot of attention for their looks, making these three the trio of 'visuals'.

Although BTS was set up to incorporate many traditional 'idol' tropes, including looking good with sharp choreography and a strong fusion of hip hop and electronic dance music, there was going to be an important difference. This band was to be real. Instead of perpetuating the 'perfect pop star' idea, the boys wanted to talk about the downsides of life for young people and were not afraid to write about their own flaws and shortcomings.

One of the early names for BTS, Bangtan Sonyeondan translates from Korean as Bulletproof Boy Scouts, which is a good example of how Bang intended his group to be different. He intended the word bulletproof to demonstrate the boys' toughness and ability to withstand the pressure. But he also thought it was important that the band was authentic and shared their real personalities with fans, as opposed to the old idea of studio idols being unrealistically perfect but unopinionated creatures. Bang wanted BTS to be relatable, frank and honest about the pressure of fame. He even imagined that perhaps the band would be able to mentor its fans. The boys of BTS were keen to travel that road. Talented enough to make their own music and lyrics they started to tell stories that their fans wanted – and were ready – to hear.

'We said what other people were feeling—like pain, anxieties and worries', said Suga. 'That was our goal, to create this empathy that people can relate to.' RM agrees, saying, 'Life has many unpredictable issues, problems, dilemmas...but I think the most important thing to live well is to be yourself. We're still trying to be us."

Their lyrics touch on themes affecting young people today, including mental health, academic stress, bullying and depression. But they have lots of positive messages as well, including how young people can find their individuality and overcome complexes and pressures, usually by 'loving oneself' – a key theme key to much of their work.

The boys have talked about trolling and bullying they have suffered themselves, for example having been wrongly accused of plagiarism and lip-synching in the past.

The boys began to spread their message in their songs and interviews, videos and, crucially, in social media updates, creating a big buzz. In December 2012, six months ahead of their official 'debut', the group, then known as the Bangtang Boys, released a couple of clips on Soundcloud. The boys were seen rapping in English and Korean, and also performing a timely cover of the Wham classic 'Last Christmas'.

By the time the seven made their official debut in 2013, renamed as BTS, they were completely prepared, preened and polished with well-rehearsed songs and slick dance routines. The band made its debut on South Korea's M Countdown K-Pop chart show, performing No More Dream from their single album 2 Cool 4 Skool.

Then on August 20, 2014, the band released its first Korean-language studio album, Dark & Wild, followed by their Japanese-language album Wake Up in 2014. Dark & Wild represented something of a shift in their sound, incorporating more hip hop and EDM.

WHY BTS?

Given that hundreds of bands make up the vibrant K-Pop scene in South Korea, what gave BTS its edge and propelled it out of its homeland to win worldwide acclaim?

As far back as 2012, Rolling Stone magazine, with its acclaimed focus on popular culture, had latched on to the fact that things happening on the South Korean music scene were about to impact the US charts. It published a list of K-Pop bands 'most likely' to crack the USA. But of course it was just a bit too early for BTS to be on the radar.

As it was, the creation of BTS was perfectly timed. The studio system was changing so that its members weren't the old-fashioned idols who were actually only popular within their own culture. Similarly the definition of masculinity in South Korea began to change so that the boys could experiment with clothes and makeup already popular in the West. Globalisation meant that cultural barriers were falling. Then of course came the impact of social media, which allowed BTS to build up a real connection with fans which undoubtedly helped to grow its fanbase.

What BTS have achieved is simply astounding. Staying true to themselves and performing music which appeals to audiences all over the world, of all races and creeds, while singing largely in Korean, BTS are truly trailblazing.

Singing predominantly in their own Korean language, BTS's first tracks were successful in their homeland and in Japan. It was their second studio album Wings in 2016 which gave the band its real break overseas. As well as selling over 1 million copies in South Korea, where it also won album of the year, it entered the American Billboard album chart at #26 and went on to become the highest-charting K-Pop record ever in the US at that time – although BTS were of course to break their own record in years to come. BTS took flight with Wings – their journey had begun.

The band scored its first number one on the World Digital Songs chart in late 2016 with Blood, Sweat & Tears from Wings, which was accompanied by an attention-grabbing gothic-style video.

BTS attends the BTS 1st Album "Dark And Wild" show Case" at the Samsung Card Hall on August 19, 2014 in Seoul, South Korea

Winning the Billboard music award for Top Social Artist chart in 2017 was another major milestone for the band and brought them worldwide attention. Their surprise win saw them beat Justin Bieber, who had won the award every year since it was created in 2011, plus other nominees, Ariana Grande, Selena Gomez and Shawn Mendes. The Social Artist award is voted for by fans and takes account of fan interactions with music, including streaming. BTS has gone on to win the award for the consecutive years since.

The other real career-changer as far as the US and UK were concerned was their third album, Love Yourself; Tear, which gave BTS their highest ever appearance in the lucrative and prestigious Western charts. Released on 18 May 2018 it made its debut at #1 on the US Billboard 200 album chart, becoming the first Korean album to top the US album chart and the highest charting album by any Asian act.

BTS performs onstage during the 2018 Billboard Music
Awards at MGM Grand Garden Arena on May 20,
2018 in Las Vegas

In the UK, Love Yourself: Tear gave BTS its highest-ever chart position, peaking at #8 in the UK album chart.

Once the Western doors were open the hits kept coming, giving BTS the distinction of becoming the fastest-selling group since The Beatles to achieve four number one albums in less than two years in America.

Following hot on the heels of the success of Love Yourself: Tear, came US number one albums Love Yourself: Answer (September 2018) Map of The Soul: Persona (April 2019) and then Map of the Soul:7 (March 2020). In the singles charts they did particularly well with their 2019 collaboration featuring Halsey, Boy With Luv which made the top 10 in the US, debuting and peaking at #8 and eventually going platinum. This track also made the top 20 in the UK, reaching #13.

Seven months into 2019, BTS had achieved five #1 hits on Billboard's World Digital Song Sales. Then in August 2020 came the jewel in the crown of the Western charts as BTS became the first Korean act to achieve a number one on both the Billboard Hot 100 singles chart, the Global 200 and the UK Official Big Top 40 with their mighty hit Dynamite. The catchy, disco-inspired track was the band's first hit to be sung in English. The music video achieved 101 million global views in 24 hours.

And of course all the while they were conquering the US and UK. their success in South Korea continued at a historic level. Having sold over 20 million albums on Korea's Gaon Music Chart, BTS became the country's best-selling artist ever, with Map of the Soul:7 the bestselling album ever at the time.

BTS took a further leap into public consciousness, outside of music fans, when Time magazine named BTS on its list of 'Next Generation Leaders'. Anybody previously unaware of K-Pop and its chart-topping supergroup received an education when the BTS boys' loomed into view on the cover of the prestigious magazine.

They were in incredible company as previous cover stars have included world leaders such as Barack Obama, acting royalty such as Tom Cruise and Nicole Kidman and other campaigning musicians such as Bono from U2. Two years later the band were named Time magazine's 'Entertainers of the Year'.

In the accompanying piece, writer Raisa Bruner described them as '.....not just the biggest K-Pop act on the charts. They've become the biggest band in the world – full stop.'

During their interview for the piece, the group spoke about their success, including their die-hard fanbase 'ARMY'.

'There are times when I'm still taken aback by all the unimaginable things that are happening. But I ask myself, "Who's going to do this, if not us?"' said Suga.

 BTS perform onstage for the 2020 American Music Awards on November 22, 2020 in South Korea

In 2017 the BTS boys began riding the crest of a wave out of South Korea and into the global music scene. The trend for exporting South Korean culture, known as Hallyu which means the Korean wave, began in the early 2000s.

Although many South Korean acts were phenomenally successful in their homeland, none had triumphantly transitioned to trouble the Western charts. With the exception of a couple of one-hit wonder novelty songs like Baby Shark by Pinkfong and Gangnam Style by Psy, Korean music didn't seem to appeal to consumers in the UK and America, who seemed largely immune to the charms of the K-Pop genre. While the first BTS tracks were successful in Korea and Japan, it took the group a couple of years to make it throughout the world. Taking their musical prowess as read, what made the difference?

MAKING

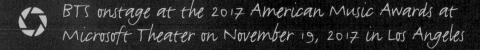

BTS onstage at the 2017 American Music Awards at Microsoft Theater on November 19, 2017 in Los Angeles

Certainly they had two things going for them which their predecessors had lacked; firstly access to the global market through YouTube and social media platforms from which they strode onto the world stage, and secondly a fan base like no other.

Then they write most of their own material, drawing on their experiences of the pressures of modern life. The boy's catchy songs include messages that are particularly relatable to their fans, especially those in their 20s and 30s.

As well as engaging seriously about the issues affecting them and their fans, BTS never forget the songs come first. Their meticulously crafted music provides a variety of tracks with monster hooks to delight their worldwide audience - everything from grand concept studio albums to more experimental singles, and from infectious pop to dreamy ballads.

MUSIC

DYNAMITE The Story of The Superstars of K-Pop

BTS

STUDIO ALBUMS

DARK AND WILD
19 August 2014

WINGS
10 October 2016

LOVE YOURSELF: TEAR
18 May 2018

MAP OF THE SOUL: 7
21 February 2020

BE
20 November 2020

50

They were also prepared to put in the work, travelling around the world to perform their songs – according to Pollstar, BTS had the sixth highest grossing tour in 2019, topping musical giants such as Ariana Grande and Paul McCartney.

BTS is one of the hardest working groups in K-Pop producing nine studio albums, four compilations, six EP's and 23 singles in their first eight years together. Alongside that all seven boys have produced solo material. By 2018 BTS had sold more than 10 million albums, setting a record for selling that many records in the shortest time of any Korean act since 2000. They are now the best-selling Korean act of all time.

The band has also released half a dozen Korean and Japanese albums, plus a number of compilation albums, reissues and EPs. Their deft touch means they are as comfortable producing high energy hip hop and electronic dance music as they are with more soulful, confessional-style ballads.

K-Pop studios are fond of re-packaging and re-releasing albums so the chronology of the music can appear a little blurred. A good way to look at BTS's output is by 'era' as they describe a particular promotional period of albums and singles connected by a theme, which progresses throughout their career.

The first three albums BTS released in Korea are known as the 'School Trilogy' and set up a 'high school bad boy' concept. The first of these albums was 2 Cool 4 Skool, in 2013, from which the band's debut single No More Dream was taken. The lyrics

BTS perform during a Korean cultural event as part of the South Korean President's official visit in France, on October 14, 2018 in Paris

are about pushing back towards a society which says young people can't follow their dreams. We Are Bullet Pt 2 was the other standout single from this album which remains very popular with fans. Then came two mini-albums O!RUL8,2? followed by Skool Luv Affair and its lead single 'Boy in Luv', both released in 2014.

Then that same year saw the release of the band's first studio album Dark & Wild which marked the end of the 'school' series as the boys transitioned into more mature song themes. Danger and War of Hormone were the standout singles from this album. It made #2 in Korea with sales of 200,000 plus.

Next came an image change as BTS emerged to promote their next series of albums, the Youth Trilogy, known also as The Most Beautiful Moment in Life (Hwa Yang Yeon Hwa in Korean so sometimes also abbreviated as HYYH). Now their style and sound was less aggressively hip hop; the boys had jettisoned their punky, bad boy look in favour of a more vulnerable and youthful look.

BTS released this HYYH music in three parts during 2015-2016 as The Most Beautiful Moment in Life Parts 1 and 2 EPs, finishing with Young Forever. The theme here was transitioning from youth to young adulthood. While this literally reflected the band members themselves growing up, critics also recognised that it marked the seven musicians moving into a more mature phase and settling into their craft. Hit singles from this period are I Need U, Dope and Run.

I Need U was the track that really changed things for BTS. It was sentimental and really appealing to a young, more mainstream audience. Billboard called it 'one of the greatest K-Pop songs of the decade'. It charted at #5 in Korea and gave them their first music show win on SBS MTV's 'The Show'. The Most Beautiful Moment in Life Pt 2 EP was their biggest hit yet, topping the weekly Korean Gaon chart and the Billboard World album chart – the first K-Pop track to do so, where it remained for 22 weeks. It also appeared on the regular Billboard album chart, peaking at #171.

V of BTS performs onstage during 102.7 KIIS FM's Jingle Ball 2019 Presented by Capital One at the Forum on December 6, 2019 in Los Angeles

2013
No More Dream
We Are Bulletproof Pt 2
N.O.

2014
Boy In Luv
Just One Day
Danger
War of Hormone

2015
I Need U (#4 on Billboard Digital)
Dope
Run

2016
Epilogue: Young Forever
Fire
Save Me
Blood Sweat & Tears

2017
Spring Day
Not Today
DNA
MIC Drop (remix, Steve Aoki and Desiigner)

2018
Fake Love
Idol

2019
Boy with Love ft Halsey
Dream Glow (with Charli XCX
A Brand New Day (with Zara Larsson)
All Night (with Juice Wrld)
Heartbeat
Make It Right ft Lauv

2020
Black Swan
ON
Dynamite
Life Goes On

53

Then came the era which really cemented the band's success– their second full studio album Wings in October 2016 which took them to the top of the Korean charts, selling 500,000 copies in its first week. Its lead single Blood Sweat and Tears topped eight charts in South Korea and its accompanying video achieved 6 million views on YouTube in 24 hours – the highest ever for a K-Pop group at the time.

This was followed by You Never Walk Alone in 2017 which was a repackage with two new singles, Not Today and Spring Day – which many fans think is one of BTS's finest ever recordings.

The Love Yourself series comprises three albums and a video telling a love story (Love Yourself: Her) , moving on to a break-up (Love Yourself: Tear) and finally a realisation that it's necessary to love yourself before you can successfully love somebody else (Love Yourself: Answer).

The release of the Love Yourself: Her album in September 2017 coincided with the band's conquering of the mainstream Western pop charts as BTS at last gained overdue recognition in the West. It spawned one of the band's most memorable

and popular singles, the catchy and fun DNA which gave BTS its first entry onto the Billboard Hot 100, coming in at #85 and rising to #67, while its accompanying music video broke the previous record for most viewed K-Pop group music video within the first 24 hours with more than 20 million YouTube views.

The follow-up single was Mic Drop (Remix) which made #28 on the Billboard Hot 100, becoming the band's first American top 40 entry as well as the first for any K-Pop artist. Both Mic Drop Remix and DNA were to be certified as Gold recordings, with Mic Drop going on to become Platinum in another first for BTS as the first Korean act with a Platinum recording.

The second album in the Love Yourself trilogy, Love Yourself: Tear, is a thematic album depicting the end of the 'Her' love affair. Its 11 tracks shift between ballads and emo pop, covering themes of love and loss. It showcased every member of the band and had a particular focus on rapping. It was critically praised with many reviewers concluding that the BTS sound had matured beautifully. The track Fake Love was a big hit from this album which provided the band with the massive achievement of its first #1 album in the US – the first K-Pop album ever to do so.

Finally comes Love Yourself: Answer which included the big hit Idol. This track had real resonance for the group. When RM sings; 'You can call me artist, you can call me idol. Or whatever else you want. I don't care,' he is commenting on the band's distain for labels and the opinions of others. It's only important that they know and love themselves. This song is also thought to be addressing the stigma attached to idol bands in Asia, similar to the opprobrium heaped upon manufactured boy bands in the west. Again this went to #1 in America.

These three commercially successful albums helped the band begin to gain international recognition. BTS broke YouTube records they had set themselves and collaborated with big Western artists including Nicki Minaj, Desiigner, and Steve Aoki.

With 2019 saw the start of the Map of the Soul recordings. First was mini-album Map of the Soul: Persona in March 2019 which provided the band with another hit single, the Boy With Luv featuring the Halsey track which gained Platinum sales and record-breaking YouTube sales.

Also from this album are Make it Right, written in collaboration with Ed Sheeran, and concert favourites Dionysus and Mikrokosmos which as polar opposite tracks are strong testament the band's depth and range which goes from heavy metal-esque to soft and emotional balladry. It was the best-selling album in South Korean history and gave the band its first #1 in the UK– the first Korean act to achieve this - and in the US, where it was the third album to top the chart in less than 12 months.

Following this would not be easy. But BTS managed it in February 2020 with the release of Map of the Soul:7 which was the band's fourth studio album. It was especially meaningful for the band because the '7' in the title had several meanings, standing for the seven members of the band, and given the fact that at this point they had been together for seven years, it was partly a memoir of their time together. Rolling Stone magazine's review of the album described it as a 'blockbuster, full of stylistic experiments that all flow together ...their most smashing album yet, showing off their mastery of different pop styles from rap bangers to prog-style philosophising'.

It features the singles Black Swan and ON and sold 4.1 million albums in its first week after release. This launched BTS into legendary status making it the best-selling act in South Korean history and again topping the charts in over 20 countries including the US, the UK, most of Europe, Australia and Canada.

Their fifth studio album Be was created during the strangest of circumstances for the world – the Covid 19 pandemic. Everything came to a halt while the world fought the virus. The boys of BTS, who had expected to spend the year on the road performing on their scheduled world tour, instead found themselves with time on their hands. They began to write about the effect of quarantine; 'the entire year got stolen' say the lyrics of Fly To My Room, although the main thrust of the album is of course, 'life must go on'. 'We call this our own "recharge" project and we hope that it will be able to recharge your own batteries, even if it's only for a moment', RM said in NME.

The track Life Goes On provided BTS with their second US number one proper in December 2020, although they had again topped the charts with a remix of Savage Love in collaboration with Jason Derulo and Jawsh in September.

BTS perform onstage during the 2018 Billboard Music Awards at MGM Grand Garden Arena on May 20, 2018 in Las Vegas

Despite their success in the US and UK album charts, until the summer of 2020 there was still an achievement which had eluded the band – a number one on the US Billboard Hot 100 and UK Top 40 singles charts. So of course they had to tick that milestone off too and did it in style with Dynamite.

The band's first English language track, Dynamite, broke records soon after it was released on 21 August 2020. As well as becoming the top-selling digital song of 2020 in the US with over 1.26 million downloads, it made number one in both the US and the UK. Its accompanying retro-style video, featuring the seven BTS boys dressed in vibrant pastel, reached 101 million views on YouTube within the first 24 hours, with more than three million fans tuning in live to watch the clip's premiere.

The upbeat track is heavily influenced by disco music, rather than the band's usual hip hop sound. Its lyrics focus on joy and appreciation for the little things that make life valuable – a message that chimed with the mood of 2020 when the world was in the grip of the Covid 19 pandemic.

BTS said they wanted the song to convey "positive vibes, energy, hope, love, purity, everything' and were reportedly in tears after hearing the track had topped the Billboard 100 singles chart – making them the first all-Korean pop act to do so.

Jimin said 'tears kept coming', adding in a tweet that he 'didn't know what to say'.

He also thanked their fans, known as ARMY, saying: 'I'm out of my mind now but you guys made this [happen].' Suga simply posted a string of crying emojis.

Dynamite reached 33.9 million US streams in its first week,

BTS onstage for the 2020 American Music Awards on November 22, 2020 in South Korea

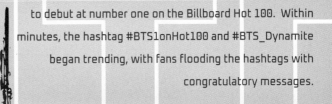

to debut at number one on the Billboard Hot 100. Within minutes, the hashtag #BTS1onHot100 and #BTS_Dynamite began trending, with fans flooding the hashtags with congratulatory messages.

Even South Korea President Moon Jae-in joined the clamour around their success, saying the boys had achieved a 'splendid feat'.

For their part the band said; 'First and foremost we give all credit to ARMY – without their support and love from Day 1 we wouldn't have come this far. Dynamite was created in the hope of bringing some vibrant energy that the world needs right now more than ever. If it made one person happier then that's more than enough for us'.

As well as its success in the UK and US, the track made the top 20 in 25 different countries around the world including Hungary, Israel, Lithuania, Malaysia, Scotland, Singapore and, of course, in the band's homeland of South Korea.

Dynamite is one of the few songs not written and produced by band members, but instead co-written by British songwriters Dave Stewart and Jessica Agombar, who got involved after hearing the band wanted to release an English language track.

Critically acclaimed around the world for its energetic and positive mood, the song was a massive hit. As The New York Times put it in their review, ' ....[while] it was less musically adventurous than the songs that made the group a worldwide phenomenon, it relies on brightness, exuberance and relentless good cheer'.

Another reviewer described the song as a 'stone-cold smash ..with one of the catchiest choruses of 2020'.

initially a standalone single, the track was later added to the album Be.

LIVE S

BTS perform onstage at the 2013 Hallyu Dream Concert on October 5, 2013 in Gyeongju, South Korea

APPEA

60

By the time BTS undertook their 2017 Wings tour they were big enough to visit a dozen countries outside Asia and include their first few concerts in America where they sold out US arenas on both coasts.

When they returned to the US during their 2018 Love Yourself World Tour they played more and larger dates. They made history in New York in October 2018 when they became the first Korean musicians to perform in a US stadium. The concert at the 40,000-seater Citi Fields in New York sold out in 10 minutes.

Reviewing the event for NME, Rhian Daly described the gig as; ' a classic stadium spectacular – a rush of slick choreography, sparkly costume changes, pyrotechnics and fireworks'

She went on to praise the fans, describing the atmosphere at the show as 'inclusive, equal and full of love ..setting an example of how to make a better world even beyond the stadium walls'.

And she perhaps found the secret of their worldwide success when she wrote that '..the rhythm of their words is often enough to pull you in even if you don't understand what they're actually saying.'

During that same tour BTS made their first visit to the UK, performing two nights at the O2 arena. Even though it was their inaugural trip, the announcement of their concerts proved the most popular show announcement ever made by the venue. The O2's tweet announcing the shows received more than 14,000 retweets and 32,000 likes, creating 949,304 impressions. Both shows sold out within an hour. And once they arrived BTS broke another record by selling more merchandise than any other act –a record held by the legendary Rolling Stones since 2012.

BTS returned to the UK the following year with two sell-out shows in June 2019 which saw them smash down another barrier as they became the first South Korean and first non-English speaking group to headline the 70,000 seat Wembley Stadium for two nights.

As RM said to the crowd; 'The UK was like a big, big wall to me. But tonight we, and you guys, just broke the wall!' And of course he thanked the fans, telling them; 'You guys are the true evidence that we are worthy to live and to keep going on.'

Suga and Jimin both agreed, telling the crowd how much Wembley had always meant to them and that it was 'the dream stage' with their appearance only made possible by fans. V spoke of his love for British culture, particularly films, songs, and fashion, while J-Hope said he was thankful to have become 'someone's love, someone's pride'.
Jin spoke of having watched the Queen biopic, Bohemian Rhapsody and he and Jungkook led the crowd in their version of Freddie Mercury's famous "ay-oh" chant, singing; 'Ey London!'

BTS perform onstage during their 1st album "Dark&Wild" showcase at Blue Square on August 19, 2014 in Seoul, South Korea.

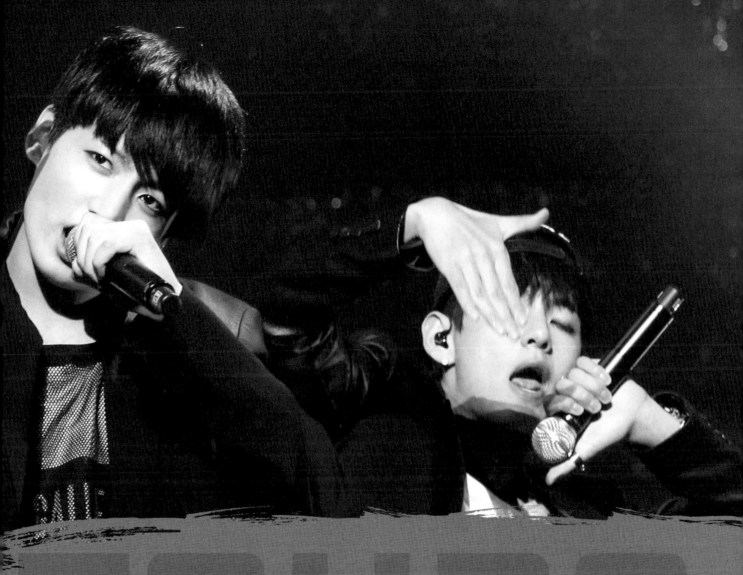

THE RED BULLET TOUR 17 October 2014 – 29 August 2015 (22 shows in Asia, Australia, North America, South America)

WAKE UP: OPEN YOUR EYES JAPAN TOUR 10 February 2015 – 19 February 2015 (6 shows in Asia)

THE MOST BEAUTIFUL MOMENT IN LIFE ON STAGE TOUR 27 November 2015 – 14 August 2016 (22 concerts in Asia)

THE WINGS TOUR 18 February 2017 – 10 December 2017 (40 concerts in Asia, South America, North America, Oceania)

LOVE YOURSELF WORLD TOUR 25 August 2018 – 29 October 2019 (62 concerts in Asia, North America, Europe, South America)

MAP OF THE SOUL WORLD TOUR scheduled for April 2020 suspended because of the coronavirus pandemic.

Dionysus

Not Today

Outro: Wings

Trivia: Just Dance
(J-Hope solo)

Euphoria
(Jungkook solo)

Best of Me

Serendipity
(Jimin solo)

Trivia: Love
(RM solo)

Boy with Luv

Dope

Silver Spoon

Fire

Idol

Singularity
(V solo)

Fake Love

Trivia: Seesaw
(Suga solo)

Epiphany
(Jin solo)

The Truth Untold
(Jin, Jimin, V and Jungkook)

Outro: Tear
(Suga, J-Hope and RM)

MIC Drop

Encore

Anpanman

So What

Make It Right

Mikrokosmos

2017 American Music Awards
rehearsals at Microsoft Theater,
November 17, 2017, Los Angeles

Aside from group performances, all the BTS boys are consummate solo showmen. They have each recorded their own material and also showcase their talents as part of the group's live shows.

On their last tour for example,

- **RM combined his rap and singing voices on the party anthem 'Love'**
- **Suga performed his smooth solo rap 'Seesaw'**
- **J-Hope showed off his high energy dancing with the track 'Just Dance'**
- **Jin sat at the piano to show off his smooth vocal range on the track 'Epiphany'**
- **Jimin danced and sang his solo pop song, 'Serendipity'**
- **V performed his smooth slow jam solo 'Singularity' alongside backup dancers in white masks in line with the concept of the track's music video**
- **Jungkook took to the air to sing the pop favourite 'Euphoria' with perfect vocals despite flying above the crowd on a zip-wire.**

In the studio the boys have worked on a variety of material from their earliest days, with RM, Suga and J-Hope all recording solo mixes.

In March 2015, RM released a single with Warren G called PDD, (Please Don't Die) ahead of his first self-titled solo mixtape RM, following it up in with Mono in 2018.

As Agust D, Suga has rapped about overcoming hate, mental health, the cost of fame and his personal struggles with depression and obsessive-compulsive disorder. J-Hope has also branched out as a rapper and had a notable solo debut in 2018 with Hope World which reached the top 40 on the Billboard 200.

Jin and V sang the original soundtrack for Hwarang the South Korean historical drama in which Jin took a supporting role.

Under BTS, Jimin has released three solo songs: Lie, Serendipity and Filter. These three solo tracks made Jimin the first South Korean artist to have hit 100 million streams on Spotify with solo material.

RM of BTS performs onstage during 102.7 KIIS FM's Jingle Ball 2019 Presented by Capital One at the Forum on December 6, 2019 in Los Angeles

BTS made its first nationally televised appearance on the US network in 2017 when they picked up their award for Best Social Artist at the Billboard Music Awards. Since then they have appeared regularly on entertainment and chat shows including; E! Entertainment Tonight, The Late Late Show with James Corden, Jimmy Kimmel Live!, The Tonight Show with Jimmy Fallon, Access Hollywood, The Ellen DeGeneres Show, America's Got Talent, Good Morning America, The Voice final and the 61st Grammy Awards Show.

In the UK they have appeared on The Graham Norton Show, Britain's Got Talent, Good Morning Britain and Lorraine, plus ITV, BBC and Sky news channels.

They come across well in interviews and are game for a laugh, having taken part in James Corden's Carpool Karaoke, as well as the 'flinch' challenge, which involves standing still while being pelted with fruit. They also took a New York subway trip with Jimmy

Fallon and performed at Grand Central Station. While RM does most of the talking as the band's leader and translator, all the boys are picking up some English phrases and can introduce themselves and understand enough to play along with most interviewers.

They performed a special MTV Unplugged session on 23 February 2021, including some unexpected versions of their hits, to great acclaim.

 BTS pose backstage in the press room for the 2017 Billboard Music Awards at the T-Mobile Arena on May 21, 2017 in Las Vegas

What the critics say ....

In her glowing review of the K-Pop band's stellar show at New York's Citi Field in October 2018 NME writer Rhian Daly paid tribute to an 'explosion of love' that saw the group emphasise the importance of kindness, inclusivity and empathy. [They are] 'the first Korean group to really break through to a worldwide audience – without using much English or kowtowing to Western trends – they exemplify the ongoing softening of pop culture, as young people utilise greater understanding of mental health and self-care than previous generations did.'

The Independent newspaper's review of BTS's October 2018 concert at the O2 described the band as part Michael Jackson, part Spice Girls, saying that .... 'BTS are the first Korean act in history to headline a British arena, and they have no intention of letting that chance go to waste...... the group skilfully dancing and singing their way through a near 30-song set list of fan favourites and album deep cuts.

There's a militancy to their tightly structured performance; one that feels so alien compared to the almost messy nature of their predecessors. Barely a beat seems to be missed, and they're performing – maybe as exaggerated versions of themselves – every minute they're on stage. Amplified for our pleasure or not, it's a glorious image that is beamed into the hearts of a K-Pop obsessed generation.'

BTS perform onstage at the 2018 Billboard Music Awards at MGM Grand Garden Arena on May 20, 2018 in Las Vegas

2017 American Music Awards rehearsals at Microsoft Theater on November 17, 2017 in Los Angeles.

2017 American Music Awards rehearsals at Microsoft Theater on November 17, 2017 in Los Angeles

A fan awaits the BTS concert as part of the "Love Yourself" North American Tour at Staples Center on September 9, 2018 in Los Angeles

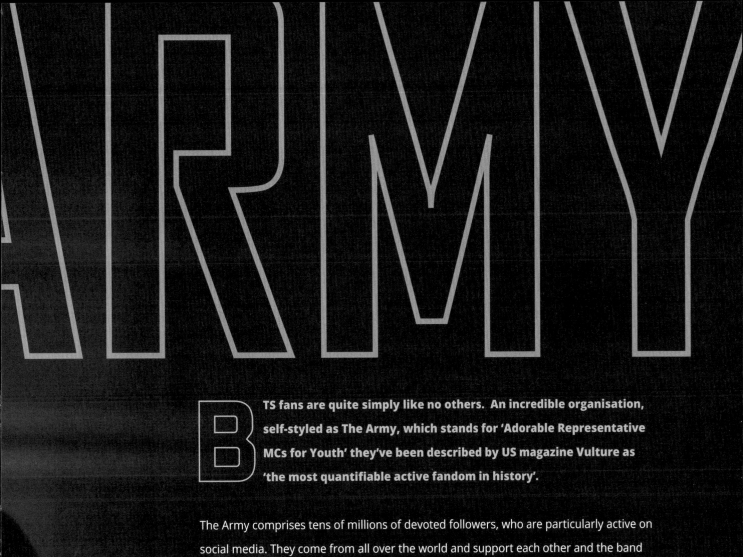

BTS fans are quite simply like no others. An incredible organisation, self-styled as The Army, which stands for 'Adorable Representative MCs for Youth' they've been described by US magazine Vulture as 'the most quantifiable active fandom in history'.

The Army comprises tens of millions of devoted followers, who are particularly active on social media. They come from all over the world and support each other and the band unreservedly. 'Even if there is a language barrier, once the music starts, people react pretty much the same wherever we go,' says Suga. 'It feels like the music really brings us together.'

What is particularly notable about The Army is its loyalty and organisational ability to mobilise to support BTS during every album, song and video release . They participate enthusiastically in online polls and ensure BTS is always trending on Twitter.

Army members camp out for hours for a glimpse of the boys ahead of concerts or TV appearances and suck up their merchandise voraciously. They use message boards, group chats and podcasts to analyse the meanings in the band's lyrics and videos, searching for messages, metaphors and cultural references. They also share stories about how BTS's music and lyrics have saved them from dark situations and helped them cope with problems and difficulties in their lives.

It was the Army that propelled the group to success and to win the 2017 Billboard Social Artist award, which first brought them to worldwide attention, and of course by buying their music the Army got them to the top of the charts. They have been compared to fans of the Beatles in the 1960s in terms of their love and devotion.

BTS regularly speak of their incredible connection with ARMY, which they have been able to maintain even during the Covid 19 pandemic for example by streaming some performances.

The band describe their fans as; 'the most passionate, the best and our motivation. They mean a lot to us. People speaking all different languages and coming from different countries, different ethnicities. It's an honour that they all listen to and enjoy our songs. It's what drives us to perform'.

The micro-blogging social media site Tumblr is dominated by BTS fans who have brought K-Pop to the fore, matching the mighty One Direction in their heyday. In April 2018, Tumblr stopped marking out K-Pop as a separate category in its popular weekly Fandom Metrics so that it could measure the relative popularity of K-Pop bands to their English language counterparts more accurately. BTS still came out at number one the first week after the categories were merged, beating both Harry Styles and Beyoncé.

The Army show their support by continuing to buy physical albums, often multiple copies, even in an age of largely digital music. They also support a huge number of BTS's brand partnerships, covering everything from cars to cosmetics.

Real die-hard BTS fans also participate in the BTS Universe, the BU, which comprises music videos, short stories, books and even a mobile game, with a cohesive narrative connection.

SOCIAL MEDIA

It's hard to underplay the effect social media has had on promotion for BTS. As RM told Time magazine, a lot of the band's success came due to the luck of the timing of their debut. The band came into its own at the same time as social media platforms like Twitter were gathering strength and platforms like the livestream service V-Live were launched. 'It was so lucky for us that social media got bigger," he said. "Uploading photos, videos, songs—now everyone does, but I think we started a little earlier, and very naturally.'

BTS first opened a Twitter account to connect with their fans in 2012 – a year before they had their first hit. So an audience was ready and eagerly waiting to hear their music.

Since that first tweet, BTS has constantly communicated with fans all around the world. They are very open with their fans, sharing minute details of their lives, outlining their creative processes, and emphasising their messages of kindness and anti-bullying to create an empathy that fans can relate to. Most importantly they never fail to acknowledge the support of their fans and to thank them for their loyalty. BTS has 23.6 million followers on Twitter and 30 million on Instagram. 300 million online votes ensured that the group won their Billboard award.

For their part, ARMY document all their interactions with the band, be it the pictures they take at their concerts or funny snapshots they turn into memes. They analyse the information from the band on fandom platforms.

Their momentum on social media has grown and grown so that in 2017 they had more likes and retweets than then US President Donald Trump and Justin Bieber combined. Every member of the band is in communication with fans all over the world, sharing everything from big news to tiny details of their daily routines.   They have also regularly shared personal vlogs to their BANGTANTV YouTube channel since their days as trainees.

BTS also has a clutch of Guinness World Records including:
- **Most Twitter engagements overall (330,624 on 21 August 2018)**
- **Fastest to reach one million followers on TikTok (3h & 31m, 23 October 2019)**
- **Most viewers for a music concert live stream (756,000 people, 14 June 2020)**
- **Most viewed YouTube music video in 24 hours by a K-Pop Group**
  (for Dynamite 21-22 August 2020 with 101.1 million views)

As RM told Time magazine 'It was so lucky for us that social media got bigger. Uploading photos, videos, songs—now everyone does, but I think we started a little earlier, and very naturally."

In February 2020 BTS broke a long standing record by achieving its 164th week at the top of the Billboard Social 50 chart, which ranks the most popular artists on Facebook, Twitter, Instagram, YouTube and Wikipedia. The chart's methodology blends weekly additions of friends/fans/followers with artist page views and engagement. The band beat the previous holder, Justin Bieber who made 163 weeks.

The BTS Army pose with photos of their idols outside the 2017 American Music Awards, November 19, 2017 at the Microsoft Theater at LA Live, in Los Angeles

BTS is one of the best-dressed boy bands in the world, known for their fashion forward looks on stage, in music videos, photoshoots and personal appearances.

From the matching dark business suits they wore at the UN General Assembly, to the more casual head to toe Celine, designed by Hedi Slimane, which the band chose for the Mnet Asian Music Awards, the seven star band members are always dressed perfectly styled for each and every occasion.

When not dressed identically, the boys co-ordinate so well, as for example when they all wore Anthony Vaccarello to the Variety magazine 'hitmaker's brunch' in Hollywood – RM, V and Jungkook in black and the others in matching suits but encrusted with sparkling crystals.

The widely admired costumes for their world tour were designed by Dior's menswear artistic director Kim Jones. His retro-futuristic designs combine masterful tailoring with technical finishes.

The starting point for the 'BTS On Tour look' was Kim Jones' autumn 2019 collection, centering on shiny and lamé fabrics. After each boy had selected his favourite look, Kim Jones worked on different designs for them all, finally presenting a selection of custom made costumes for them to choose from.

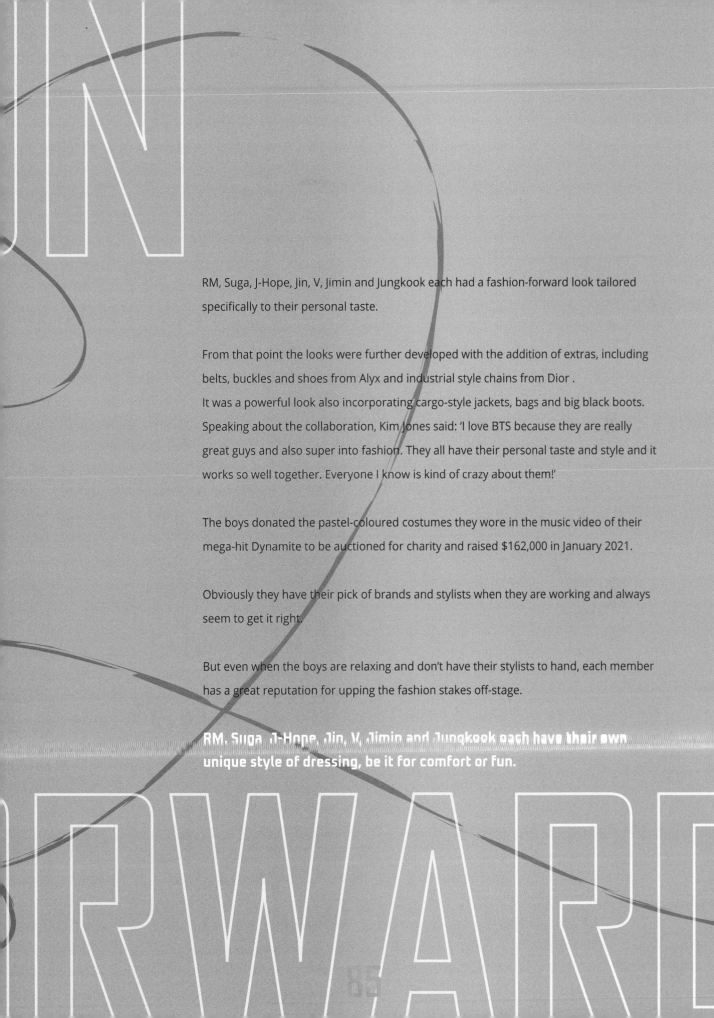

RM, Suga, J-Hope, Jin, V, Jimin and Jungkook each had a fashion-forward look tailored specifically to their personal taste.

From that point the looks were further developed with the addition of extras, including belts, buckles and shoes from Alyx and industrial style chains from Dior .
It was a powerful look also incorporating cargo-style jackets, bags and big black boots.
Speaking about the collaboration, Kim Jones said: 'I love BTS because they are really great guys and also super into fashion. They all have their personal taste and style and it works so well together. Everyone I know is kind of crazy about them!'

The boys donated the pastel-coloured costumes they wore in the music video of their mega-hit Dynamite to be auctioned for charity and raised $162,000 in January 2021.

Obviously they have their pick of brands and stylists when they are working and always seem to get it right.

But even when the boys are relaxing and don't have their stylists to hand, each member has a great reputation for upping the fashion stakes off-stage.

RM, Suga, J-Hope, Jin, V, Jimin and Jungkook each have their own unique style of dressing, be it for comfort or fun.

Press conference marking the release of its new album "Map of the Soul Persona" at Dongdaemun Design Plaza in central Seoul on April 17, 2019 in Seoul, South Korea

RM's style has changed dramatically since his days with Korea's underground rap scene. He is good at experimenting with different pieces which others might not think of putting together.

He loves streetwear in general, and Japanese streetwear in particular. When he's not working he likes a strong look and is often seen wearing the bright colours of pieces from Japanese label WTAPS. He's king of the 'jort' (shorts made like cut-off jeans) and often seen in such denim shorts from Visvim. He's fond of wearing shorts generally and often teams them up with a matching short-sleeved shirt.

Favourite Brands: Yohji, Y-3, WTAPS, Neighbourhood, Visvim

Suga's style is more reserved than many of the BTS members and involves a lot of black and leather.

He'll often be spotted combining the two in a top-quality leather jacket, or overcoat, matched with a plain black shirt and black denim jeans. Think dark muted tones and soft cosy fabrics to get Suga's look. Like Jin, he enjoys an over-sized top. He likes to stay warm and is fond of a hat. Mastermind Japan is one of his favourite brands, which he often teams with high-end designer accessories.

Favourite Brands: Mastermind Japan, Visvim, Gucci, Balenciaga, Saint Laurent.

The BTS dance king J-Hope often rocks a cap, a bucket hat or a bandana as his 'crown'. To match his personality, J-Hope's look is 'out there', colourful and bold.

Streetwear is one of his favourite 'off-duty' looks – both sporty and high end. Like his fellow rapper friend RM, J-Hope can pull off some unconventional combinations and enjoys wearing shorts of all varieties. He is often seen with a bag of some description – anything from a snazzy satchel to a small purse.

Favourite Brands: Raf Simons, YEEZY, Louis Vuitton, JW Anderson, Off-White

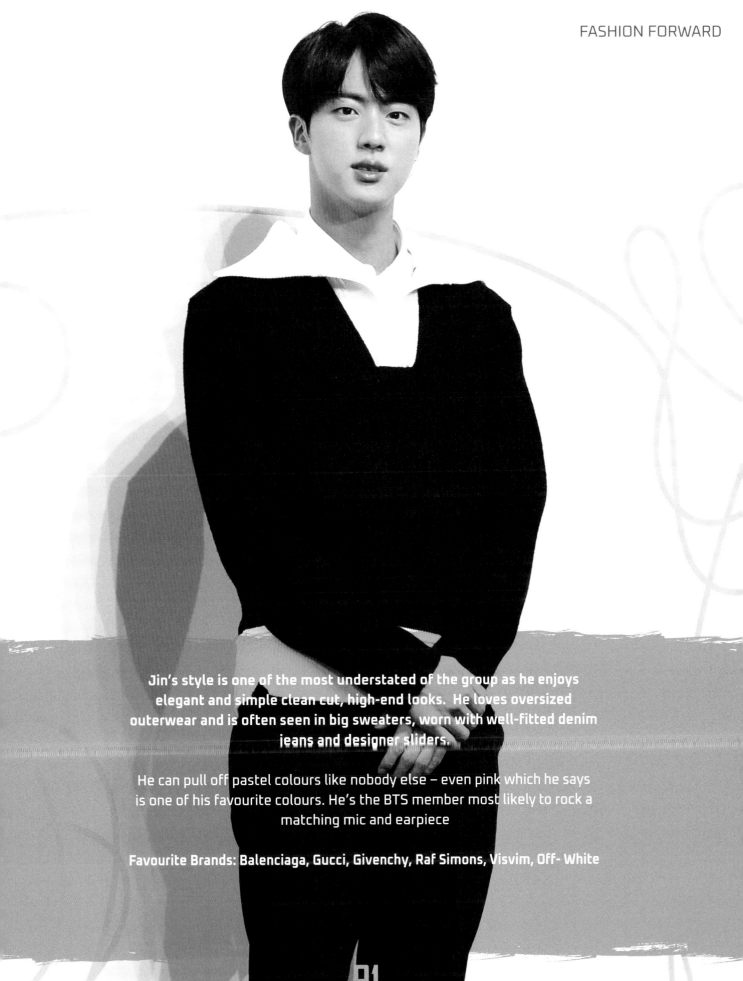

Jin's style is one of the most understated of the group as he enjoys elegant and simple clean cut, high-end looks. He loves oversized outerwear and is often seen in big sweaters, worn with well-fitted denim jeans and designer sliders.

He can pull off pastel colours like nobody else – even pink which he says is one of his favourite colours. He's the BTS member most likely to rock a matching mic and earpiece

Favourite Brands: Balenciaga, Gucci, Givenchy, Raf Simons, Visvim, Off- White

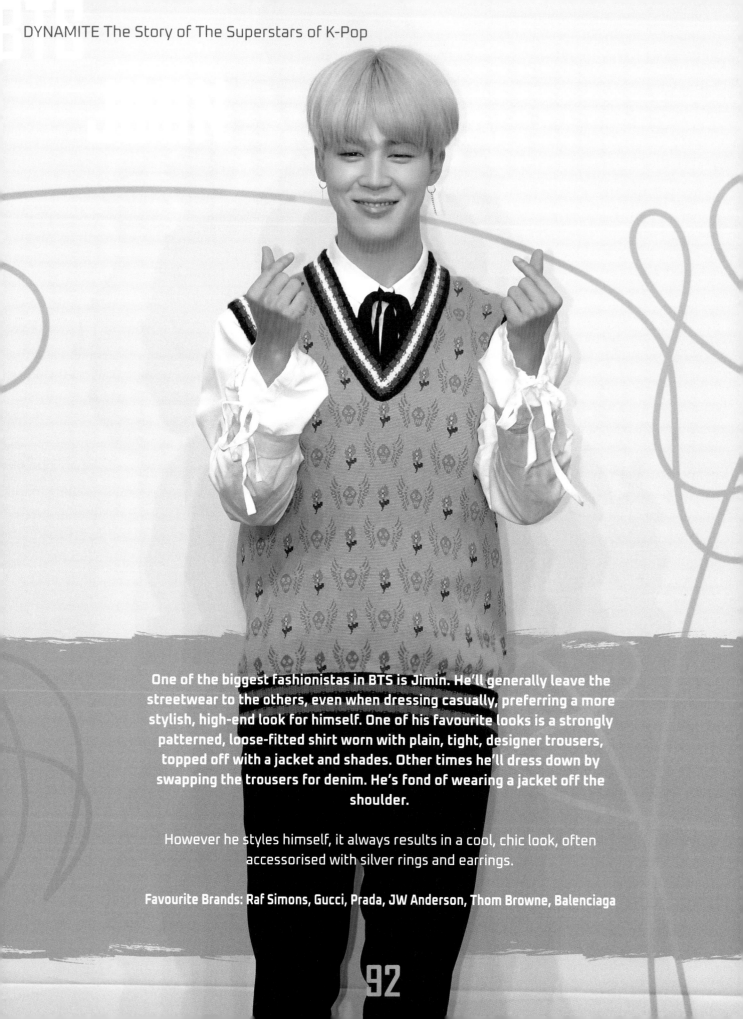

One of the biggest fashionistas in BTS is Jimin. He'll generally leave the streetwear to the others, even when dressing casually, preferring a more stylish, high-end look for himself. One of his favourite looks is a strongly patterned, loose-fitted shirt worn with plain, tight, designer trousers, topped off with a jacket and shades. Other times he'll dress down by swapping the trousers for denim. He's fond of wearing a jacket off the shoulder.

However he styles himself, it always results in a cool, chic look, often accessorised with silver rings and earrings.

Favourite Brands: Raf Simons, Gucci, Prada, JW Anderson, Thom Browne, Balenciaga

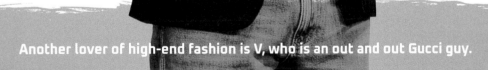

Another lover of high-end fashion is V, who is an out and out Gucci guy.

He rocks a wide-flowing trouser teamed with a silk, button up shirt, accessorised with simple jewellery and dress shoes. Sometimes in all black and other times with bolder patterns and colours, he has found a style that suits him and sticks with it more times than not. He's not particularly experimental in his choices and generally wouldn't look out of place in any fashion magazine. Outside of Gucci, and for a more casual day, V likes a loose-fitting sweatshirt and pants and likes to pull everything together with long coats in neutral colours. Mis-matched earrings are his style quirk.

Favourite Brands: Gucci, Louis Vuitton, Hermes, Burberry

He's the youngest of the BTS boys but doesn't let that hold him back fashion-wise, managing to stand out among his stylish, older bandmates.

He's moving on from his old beloved look of white t-shirt and Timberland boots to now take on some more striking looks. He likes wearing button-up Gucci or Prada shirts, often paired with Calvin Klein jeans. Labels such as WTAPS and Visvim feature in his casual wardrobe where he likes to combine practicality with style, enjoying oversized hoodies and beanie hats.

Favourite Brands: Gucci, WTAPS, Calvin Klein, Raf Simons, Monitaly

95

As well as spreading messages of love, BTS are quick to back up their words with deeds and are known to support countless charities. The loyal fans who form the BTS Army are never far behind. In June 2020 the BTS ARMY mobilised to match a $1m donation by the group to the Black Lives Matter movement. Once word of the donation reached fans, the hashtag #MatchAMillion began trending on Twitter, to raise the same amount again.

Within the first 24 hours the collection had passed $817,000. 'One In An Army', the fan collective behind the donation drive, said 'We stand in solidarity with black ARMY. They're an important part of our family. And we stand with black people everywhere. Your voices deserve to be heard."

BTS's social media following is known for its devotion and activism and had already organised online protests in support of Black Lives Matter.

BTS began their charitable endeavours back in 2015, by donating seven tons of rice to charity in South Korea and their good works haven't stopped since, particularly for poverty relief charities. In addition:
In 2016 they worked to raise donations for LISA, a Korean medical charity which promotes organ and blood donation.

In January 2017, BTS and Big Hit Entertainment donated more than $85,000 to a charity set up to support the families affected by the sinking of the MV Sewol ferry in South Korea which cost more than 300 lives.

Later that year, BTS officially launched its Love Myself campaign, partnering with the Korean Committee for UNICEF's #ENDviolence campaign dedicated to funding several social programs to prevent violence against children and teens and to provide support for victims of violence. BTS members donated personally and also via a percentage of album sales. In its first six months alone donations totalled US$1.4 million and have continued to rise steadily ever since.

In September 2018, BTS supported the United Nation's launch of its youth initiative 'Youth 2030', intended to provide quality education and training for young people (see box). BTS were asked to champion this initiative because of their reach within the 15-25 year olds demographic and their acknowledged impact on youth culture through their music and social messages.

In January 2020, the band partnered with Starbucks Korea for the 'Be the Brightest Stars' campaign which saw a proportion of profits from limited-edition drinks, food and merchandise going towards career and educational development programs for disadvantaged youngsters.

A set of seven microphones used by the band during the Love Yourself World Tour were auctioned as part of the Grammy week charity auction and achieved the highest bid of the whole event, raising US$83,000 for MusiCares.

Personally, and usually privately, members of BTS donate to charities of special interest to them. Here are just a few of the donations which have leaked into the public domain;

RM donated over 100 million Korean Won (equivalent to US$88,000) to the Seoul Samsung School which specialises in educating hearing-impaired children.

Suga has donated beef to 39 orphanages and foster homes and US$88,000 to the Korea Paediatric Cancer Foundation.

J-Hope has donated around US$200,000 to date to Child Fund Korea, in support of his old high school. He also donated another US$90,000 in support of children experiencing economic difficulties following the Covid-19 pandemic.

Jin is a member of South Korea's Honor's Club which means he makes monthly donations totalling at least US $88,000 a year

Jimin also supported his old school Busan Hodong Elementary School by covering uniform expenses and in 2019 he donated around US$ 88,000 to the Busan Department of Education to help support lower income students. In July 2020, Jimin donated another US$88,000 to the Jeonnam Future Education Foundation, for the creation of a scholarship fund for talented, but financially struggling, students.

The ARMY is also a formidable force for good, regularly donating to charity in the name of the group and it's individual members. For example on Jungkook's birthday fans donated to various causes including We Purple Rain, raising enough money to plant more than 8,000 trees in the Amazon Rainforest.

 BTS perform during a Korean cultural event as part of South Korean president official visit in France, on October 14, 2018 in Paris

In 2018, BTS became the first K-Pop group to speak at the United Nations to support the launch of the UN's Generation Unlimited, a youth empowerment initiative aimed at improving career education and training for young people worldwide.

Speaking at the UN General Assembly in New York on 24 September 2018, RM spoke about the importance of self-acceptance, saying; 'No matter who you are or where you're from, your skin colour, your gender identity, speak yourself."

"We have learned to love ourselves. So now, I urge you to speak yourself. I'd like to ask all of you, 'What is your name?'" RM, the group's leader, said. "I want to hear your voice, and I want to hear your conviction. No matter who you are, where you're from, your skin colour, gender identity, just speak yourself."

RM'S SPEECH TO THE UN IN FULL

'Thank you, Mr Secretary General, UNICEF Executive Director, Excellencies and distinguished guests from across the world.

'My name is Kim Nam Jun, also known as RM, the leader of the group BTS. It's an incredible honour to be invited to an occasion with such significance for today's young generation.

'Last November, BTS launched the 'Love Myself' campaign with UNICEF, building on our belief that 'true love first begins with loving myself.' We have been partnering with UNICEF's #ENDviolence program to protect children and young people all over the world from violence.

'Our fans have become a major part of this campaign with their action and enthusiasm. We truly have the best fans in the world!

'I would like to begin by talking about myself.

'I was born in Ilsan, a city near Seoul, South Korea. It's a beautiful place, with a lake, hills, and even an annual flower festival. I spent a happy childhood there, and I was just an ordinary boy.

'I would look up at the night sky in wonder and dream the dreams of a boy. I used to imagine that I was a superhero, saving the world.

'In an intro to one of our early albums, there is a line that says, "My heart stopped...I was maybe nine or ten."

'Looking back, that's when I began to worry about what other people thought of me and started seeing myself through their eyes. I stopped looking up at the stars at night. I stopped daydreaming. I tried to jam myself into moulds that other people made. Soon, I began to shut out my own voice and started to listen to the voices of others. No one called out my name, and neither did I. My heart stopped and my eyes closed shut. So, like this, I, we, all lost our names. We became like ghosts.

'I had one sanctuary, and that was music. There was a small voice in me that said, "Wake up, man, and listen to yourself!" But it took me a long time to hear music calling my name.

'Even after making the decision to join BTS, there were hurdles. Most people thought we were hopeless. Sometimes, I just wanted to quit.

'I think I was very lucky that I didn't give it all up.

'I'm sure that I, and we, will keep stumbling and falling. We have become artists performing in huge stadiums and selling millions of albums.

'But I am still an ordinary, twenty-four-year-old guy. If there's anything that I've achieved, it was only possible because I had my other BTS members by my side, and because of the love and support of our ARMY fans.

'Maybe I made a mistake yesterday, but yesterday's me is still me. I am who I am today, with all my faults. Tomorrow I might be a tiny bit wiser, and that's me, too. These faults and mistakes are what I am, making up the brightest stars in the constellation of my life. I have come to love myself for who I was, who I am, and who I hope to become.

'I would like to say one last thing.

'After releasing the "Love Yourself" albums and launching the "Love Myself" campaign, we started to hear remarkable stories from our fans all over the world, how our message helped them overcome their hardships in life and start loving themselves. These stories constantly remind us of our responsibility.

'So, let's all take one more step. We have learned to love ourselves, so now I urge you to "speak yourself."

'I would like to ask all of you. What is your name? What excites you and makes your heart beat?

'Tell me your story. I want to hear your voice, and I want to hear your conviction. No matter who you are, where you're from, your skin colour, gender identity: speak yourself.

'Find your name, find your voice by speaking yourself.

'I'm Kim Nam Jun, RM of BTS.

'I'm a hip hop idol and an artist from a small town in Korea.

'Like most people, I made many mistakes in my life.

'I have many faults and I have many fears, but I am going to embrace myself as hard as I can, and I'm starting to love myself, little by little.

'What is your name? Speak Yourself!'

WINI

BTS are certainly winning at life at the moment – all conquering as musicians and influencers.

As well as being featured on Time magazine's international cover as 'Next Generation Leaders', BTS have also appeared in the magazines lists of the 25 most influential people on the internet (2017–2019) and on the 100 most influential people in the world (2019).

Forbes Korea ranked BTS as the most influential celebrities in the country in 2018 and 2020, and the band was also ranked 43rd in the Forbes Celebrity 100 in 2019, putting them among the top-earning celebrities in the world.

Their success has propelled Big Hit Entertainment, the small studio which launched them, into the big time. Big Hit is now one of the most valuable entertainment entities in South Korea and went public on the Korean KOSPI stock exchange in October 2020 with an initial valuation of US$4.1 billion.

BTS attends the 61st Annual GRAMMY Awards at Staples Center on February 10, 2019 in Los Angeles

In 2019, BTS was said to be worth more than $4.65 billion to South Korea's economy each year – that equates to 0.3 percent of the country's GDP. The country believes that BTS attract one in every 13 foreign tourists to the country and cites them as a key act responsible for boosting global music sales to $19 billion in 2018.

According to Forbes, they earned $50m last year, with their road show grossing $170m.

But by some measures, their contribution to South Korea's economy is far bigger. One recent study by the tourism ministry and a government tourism institute calculated that their single Dynamite alone would generate a staggering $2.4bn in economic activity and nearly 8,000 new jobs - coming not just from direct sales but from sales of linked cosmetics, food and drink.

So it's perhaps unsurprising that every member of the band has been awarded the Order of Cultural Merit by the President of South Korea – making them the youngest ever recipients of the award which is given for outstanding contributions in spreading Korean culture and language around the world.

Their homeland holds the boys in such high esteem that it has even made a change to the law to exempt them from military service until the age of 30. In Korea all able-bodied men aged between 18 and 28 must serve two years in the military. In the past exceptions were only made for high-profile Olympic sports stars, but now following a recommendation from the culture minister, entertainers, including pop stars BTS, can delay signing up to serve. The change comes in recognition of their contribution towards boosting the South Korean economy and popularising the country's culture around the world.

These seven boys from South Korea, working together as BTS, have smashed down music barriers to take the US, UK and the rest of the world by storm. As well as being talented and respectful they have always stayed true to themselves. They only produced a much requested English-language song once they had already conquered the world in their mother-tongue.

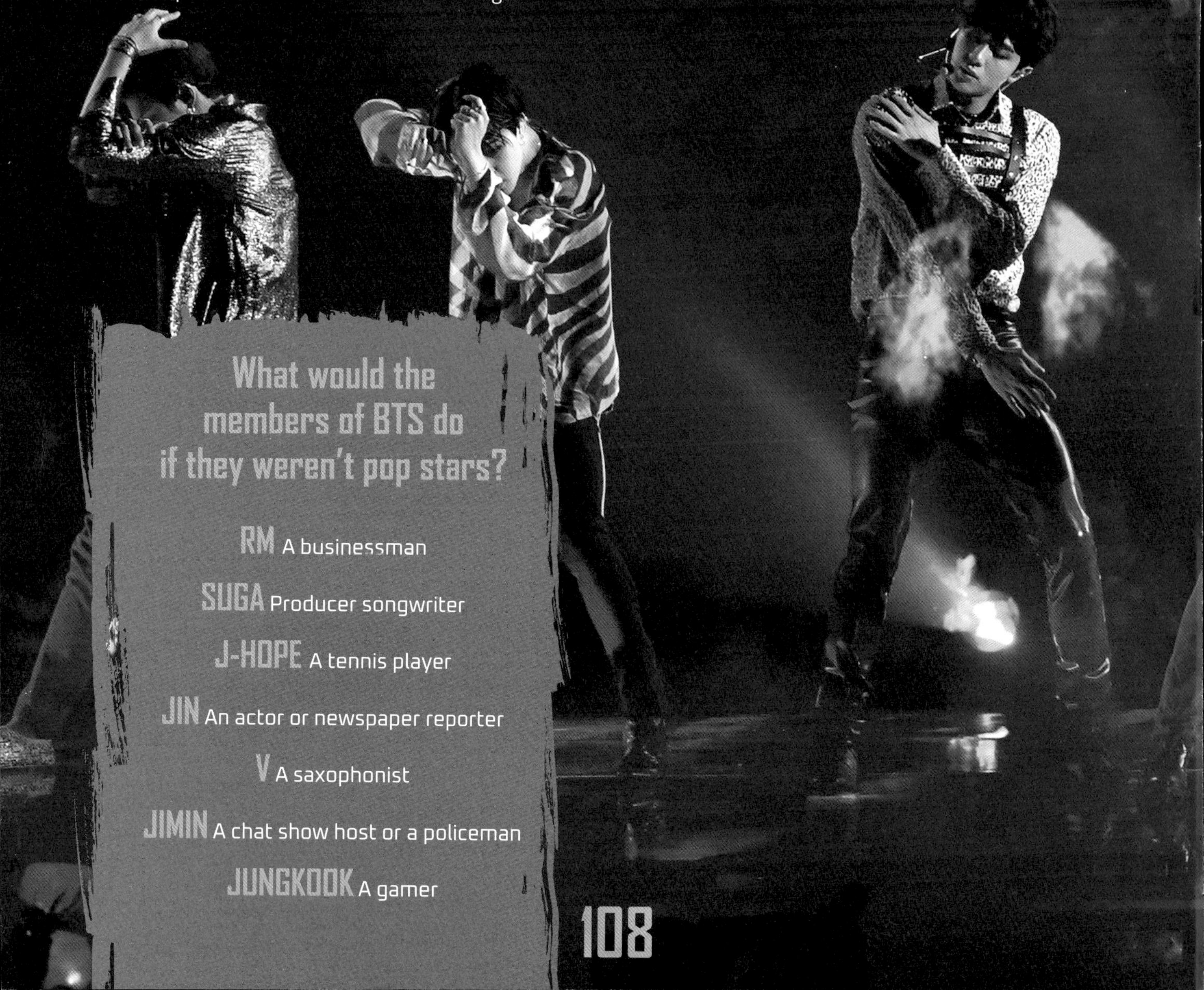

What would the members of BTS do if they weren't pop stars?

RM A businessman

SUGA Producer songwriter

J-HOPE A tennis player

JIN An actor or newspaper reporter

V A saxophonist

JIMIN A chat show host or a policeman

JUNGKOOK A gamer

BTS' hard work and talent is undeniable. Their on-point vocals and precise dance moves are flawless thanks to constant practice. The boys have creative control and write and produce many of their own songs.

But notwithstanding their huge talent and success, they remain humble and thankful to fans which all adds to their huge appeal. Preaching love, understanding and peace and bringing great joy to their fans, BTS simply describe themselves as 'boys from Korea who love music and performing'.

To give BTS the last word, they say they would like to be remembered as; 'Seven boys who are sincere in their craft, in their lyrics, and in their actions'.

BTS perform onstage during the 2018 Billboard Music Awards at MGM Grand Garden Arena on May 20, 2018 in Las Vegas